SOUL
SAMURAI

Qui Nguyen

Broadway Play Publishing Inc
224 E 62nd St, NY, NY 10065
www.broadwayplaypub.com
info@broadwayplaypub.com

SOUL SAMURAI
©2010 by Qui Nguyen

First printing: June 2010
Second printing: June 2011
I S B N: 978-0-88145-451-2

Book design: Marie Donovan
Typography/page layout: Adobe InDesign
Typeface: Palatino
Printed and bound in the U S A

ORIGINAL PRODUCTION

SOUL SAMURAI was first produced by Ma-Yi Theater (Ralph Pena, Artistic Director; Jorge Ortoll, Executive Director; Suzette Porte, Producer) and Vampire Cowboys (Abby Marcus, Producer) at HERE Arts Center (N Y C) in February/March 2009. The cast and contributors were:

Dewdrop, Angela	Maureen Sebastian
Cert, T-Bone, Avory, Online	Paco Tolson
Boss 2K, Fang, Burngout, Marcus, Master Leroy	Sheldon Best
Sally, Lady Snowflake	Bonnie Sherman
Grandmaster Mack, Hurt, Neutral Mask Marcus, Kane, Pastor, Stranger	Jon Hoche

Director ....Robert Ross Parker
Scenic/lighting designer ....Nick Francone
Costume designer ....Sarah Laux & Jessica Wegener
Sound designer .... Sharath Patel
Puppet design/construction ....David Valentine
Fight direction ....Qui Nguyen
Production stage managers ....Lydsey Goode & Kat West
Assistant stage manager ....Danielle Buccino
Production manager .... Gregg Bellon
Crew ... Pete Boisvert, Stephanie Cox Williams, Matthew Tennie, Charles Timko
Publicity/press rep ....Jim Baldassare
Photographers .... Jim Baldassare, Theresa Squire

CHARACTERS & SETTING

1. DEWDROP, ANGELA
2. CERT, T-BONE, AVORY, ONLINE
3. BOSS 2K, FANG, BURNOUT, MARCUS, MASTER LEROY
4. SALLY, LADY SNOWFLAKE
5. GRANDMASTER MACK, HURT, NEUTRAL MASK
   MARCUS, KANE, PASTOR, STRANGER

Note: All actors play random gang members when needed

Post-apocalyptic N Y C

ACT ONE

Prologue

(Projection: "Soul: The spiritual nature of human beings, regarded as immortal, separable from the body at death, and susceptible to happiness or misery in a future state.")

(Projection: "Samurai: One bad mutha...")

(Projection: "Shut yo' mouth!")

(A smooth riff begins playing...)

(Lights come up in the middle of a fight between BOSS 2K, *A larger than life badass gangboss, and* CERT, *a young but feisty b-boy armed with a wooden samurai sword.)*

BOSS 2K: Yo suckah, you messin' with the wrong muthafuckah, you dig?

CERT: Partna, the only thing I'm gonna be digging is gonna be yo' grave.

(Projection: "Location: Coney Island, Brooklyn")

BOSS 2K: I'm gonna have fun fucking you the fuck up.

(CERT bravely attacks.)

(BOSS 2K, however, with some slick moves knocks CERT down.)

BOSS 2K: Yo' stupid ass ain't even knowing what you just walked into. Brooklyn is Long Tooth territory. You best recognize.

CERT: Naw, Jack. Only sap here gonna be takin' a dirt nap is gonna be yo' ugly ass.

BOSS 2K: Talk mighty big for a little man.

CERT: Well, I gots a surprise, bitch.

BOSS 2K: And what's that? You gonna bleed all over my nice kicks some more?

(DEWDROP, *a smooth Asian-American lady samurai, appears onto stage.*)

DEWDROP: Nope. Yo' ass is just gonna die.

BOSS 2K: And who the fuck is you?

DEWDROP: I'm the surprise bitch.

(BOSS 2K *smiles. He raises the weapon he just took away from* CERT. *She raises a katana. He attacks her.* DEWDROP, *however, is too quick and stabs him through Samurai-style. Blood gushes out of his wound. He falls.*)

CERT: Dammmmmmmmmmmn! See, nobody messes with the Cert and the Dewdrop. I told you, we'ze the baddest, we'ze the prettiest, we'ze the G D finest!

DEWDROP: The fuck you doing, bozu?

CERT: I'm talking smack. Talking smack is the best part.

DEWDROP: I know something more fun.

CERT: And what's that, fly girl?

(DEWDROP *tosses* CERT *her sword.*)

DEWDROP: Cut off his head.

CERT: Say what?

DEWDROP: Cut off his muthafuckin' head. We gotsa roll.

CERT: Yo, why do I gotsa do clean-up? I ain't the one who made the mess.

DEWDROP: Cause you're my sidekick, bozu. That's yo' job.

CERT: Fuck that. I ain't nobody's sidekick. If anything, you're my muhfuckin' sidekick.

DEWDROP: Just get it.

CERT: Yo, how much time we got til sun up?

DEWDROP: Eight hours.

CERT: Eight hours! That's a long time, yo.

DEWDROP: I ain't the one who went in with guns all a'blazing without a plan, now was I?

CERT: Muhfuckah was right there! What was I gonna do?

(We hear the sounds of bottle breaking in the background.)

CERT: The fuck was that?

(We hear dozens of LONG TOOTH gang-members approaching.)

DEWDROP: Well, hell, that didn't take long.

CERT: Long Tooths?

DEWDROP: Who else gonna be walking these streets this late?

CERT: How far are we from Manhattan?

DEWDROP: About twenty miles.
We need to book.

CERT: What about the head?

DEWDROP: Fuck the head—he's dead. It's time for Plan B, yo.

CERT: What's that?

DEWDROP: Run.

(They exit!)

(As they do, LONG TOOTHS enter the stage. They see the

fallen BOSS 2K. *They run after* CERT *and* DEWDROP.)

(Cut to...)

(Slo-mo movement sequence: DEWDROP *and* CERT *running for their lives away from* LONG TOOTHS *to music like Isaac Hayes' "Shaft" Theme.)*

(Projection: [Producing Company]
Projection: Presents
Projection: SOUL SAMURAI
Projection: A Vampire Cowboys Creation)

(Blackout)

One

(Projection: CHAPTER ONE: DEALS MADE IN BLOOD ALWAYS RUN...)

DEWDROP: *(Addressing the audience)* Moshi, moshi, muthafuckahs. Welcome to the middle of my story. Welcome to the penultimate moment in my demise. As you can see, we're not doing so good. The kinda angry, kinda pissed off, kinda evil sonofagun we just whacked was the old Boss 2K. He's a bad guy. I'm not gonna lie—we ain't exactly boyscouts either. We're now on the run to get back home—back to the N Y C, back to the Apple—however...

   Let's do a bit of a rewind first, shall we? A storied death without context has about as much meaning as bumping uglies without orgasm. Before we can get this story a pumpin', let's warm up your naughty parts first...

(Projection: One week earlier)

(Projection: Lower East Side, Manhattan)

(Lights come up on GRANDMASTER MACK, *the Shogun of Manhattan [and, yeah, he's a straight up pimp, yo]. He has a*

hot harem girl, WHITE CHOCOLATE, draped at his side.)

(FANG, a large sized bodyguard, brings in DEWDROP.)

GRANDMASTER MACK: Now what do we have here?

FANG: Grandmaster Mack, sir.

GRANDMASTER MACK: Just a hot second, suckah. Let me soak this in. That's one nice slice you got there. Ain't seen a piece so sweet in these parts in some time.

FANG: Sir.

GRANDMASTER MACK: Now what is a fine little mama like yourself doing down here in the L.E.S.?

FANG: SIR!

GRANDMASTER MACK: What, fool? What?

(DEWDROP shows that she's holding a katana against FANG's neck.)

FANG: She's sporting Japanese steel.

GRANDMASTER MACK: Well, ain't that's some slick shit.

DEWDROP: Slick and sharp.

GRANDMASTER MACK: You took down Fang?

DEWDROP: Is it his sword at my neck?

GRANDMASTER MACK: You must got some moves.

DEWDROP: Like Solid Gold.

GRANDMASTER MACK: Who are you?

DEWDROP: My name's Dewdrop. I live in the lowdown.

GRANDMASTER MACK: I ain't askin' bout your tag, Turkey. I'm askin' who you are? What colors you fly?

DEWDROP: My own.

GRANDMASTER MACK: Hm. You are one interesting lil kitty.

DEWDROP: I'm a kitty who's done spent more than a

few of her nine lives keeping dogs out her litter.

GRANDMASTER MACK: *(Pointing to her Katana)* Is that what you're doing with that *yaiba*?

DEWDROP: This *yaiba* is my boy-toy. You wanna see what happens when someone tries to step in between? We get very jealous.

GRANDMASTER MACK: You're a cute clever little bitch, you know that?

DEWDROP: Call me a bitch again and you'll see exactly how sharp my wit can be.

GRANDMASTER MACK: So what's your bag? Why are you here?

DEWDROP: I want passage into the badlands.

GRANDMASTER MACK: You want what?

DEWDROP: To get into the badlands.

GRANDMASTER MACK: I heard you the first time. You crazy?

DEWDROP: I got business there. Needs handlin'.

GRANDMASTER MACK: Where?

DEWDROP: The fairgrounds.

GRANDMASTER MACK: You're a funny little rabbit. You straight-up fucked in the head, but you funny.

DEWDROP: I'm not joking.

GRANDMASTER MACK: Coney Island is Boss 2K territory. I'm talking Long Tooths. That's one badass gang.

DEWDROP: I ain't here to wax philosophy. I'm here to get a pass. You control the bridge, I need entrance.
   The only peeps that get to cross wear your colors. Everybody knows that.

GRANDMASTER MACK: You want to be one of my fine

black assassins?

DEWDROP: I want to get to the coast. And if wearing your colors helps me do that, then I'm gonna wear your colors.

GRANDMASTER MACK: That doesn't make for a convincing argument to be employed.

DEWDROP: I'm not looking for employment, Grandmaster Mack. I'm just looking for style.

GRANDMASTER MACK: Now you really are talking crazy. No way.

I let a lowdowner like you into the badlands wearing black, that'll draw me some dirty looks. Not just from the Long Tooths, but from my own crew too. It's gonna take more than an idle threat for me to put up with that.

However... if you want to barter something other than words... well, lookin' at that fine body of yours—

DEWDROP: Try to step. See what kinda crazy I can get.

GRANDMASTER MACK: You should go home, yella girl. I'm sorry to inform you. But as it turns out, there's no applications available here. Sorry.

DEWDROP: You have to help me.

GRANDMASTER MACK: I ain't have to do shit.

DEWDROP: I'll slice open your boy here. I mean it.

GRANDMASTER MACK: Go ahead. He owes me money anyhow.

FANG: Sir...

DEWDROP: You'd really let him die?

GRANDMASTER MACK: I'm a shogun, sister. Shoguns don't bow to nobody.

(DEWDROP *rears back her sword.*)

FANG: AAAAAAAAAGH!

(GRANDMASTER MACK does not budge.)

(DEWDROP, however, does not kill FANG.)

GRANDMASTER MACK: I guess you aren't nearly as tough as you thought you were.

DEWDROP: Fuck you. *(Starts to exit.)*

GRANDMASTER MACK: Stop.

(DEWDROP pauses.)

GRANDMASTER MACK: Do you really want to sport my colors?

DEWDROP: Yes.

GRANDMASTER MACK: Then I have a bargain for you. If you want in—you gotta do me a job. I'll give you time to die inside, but you gotta dance for me. Understood?

DEWDROP: What is it?

GRANDMASTER MACK: I need you to knock off the Kingsborough King.

DEWDROP: You want me to kill Boss 2K?

GRANDMASTER MACK: Yep.

DEWDROP: That's funny.

GRANDMASTER MACK: Why's that, little rabbit?

DEWDROP: That's the reason I wanna go there in the first place.

(Cut to...)

(Lights up on CERT at a street corner.)

CERT: So what'd he say?

DEWDROP: I'm in.

CERT: That's my girl! That's my girl!

DEWDROP: Yo, why the hell are you so happy?

CERT: Cause I'm ready for some action, yo. That's why.

Open a can on some fucked up muthafuckahs. Get my man on. Show'em what's the what's up.

DEWDROP: You're not coming with me.

CERT: Yo, say what?

DEWDROP: You're not coming with me.

CERT: But we're a team. The Cert and the Dewdrop. The heavy and the hotness. The Boy Badass and the Lady Samurai!

DEWDROP: The boy badass?

CERT: Yo, you need some back. Check it, I even got me a sword! (*He pulls out a long wooden samurai sword hidden in his baggie pants.*)

DEWDROP: It's made out of wood.

CERT: It'll come in handy.

DEWDROP: Damon.

CERT: Cert.

DEWDROP: Cert, this shit is screwed with a capital "F". I'm talkin' fuckin' fucked up mothafuckahs are gonna be jacked up ready to come a killin' as soon as I cross that bridge. Long Tooth gangbangers and Brooklyn bustas out for blood. Yo, I sport black just to get past the bridge, but black don't mean black in Brooklyn. These colors only got power in Manhattan. Over in the badlands, being able to kill is cash and yo' ass is broke. Sides, what I gotta do is messy. You don't want to jump into this and get my stink all over you.

CERT: Yo, you ain't stinky? You smell good.

DEWDROP: Get off me, fool, I'm serious. What I got to do ain't for you.

CERT: You sayin' you bullet proof now?

DEWDROP: In Brooklyn, I ain't got to worry about bullets.

CERT: That's not what I'm implying. I'm asking you straight—are you indestructible?

DEWDROP: I can hold my own.

CERT: Not against them you can't. I used to live in the badlands, baby. Long Tooths ain't just hype. They'll fuck you up proper. Fo' real.

DEWDROP: I know that.

CERT: Then you need some back.

DEWDROP: I'm going there to do some killing, Cert. You really want that kinda blood on your hands? I'm talking gallons. This beef I got runs deep.

CERT: I know all about—

DEWDROP: No, you don't. Those Long Tooths took something important from me. I plan on paying them back my pain with interest. You dragging along is just gonna give me conscience. I don't need that for what I gotta do.

CERT: Dewdrop...

DEWDROP: No! (*Cut to... Addressing the audience*) Oh right... you might wanna know what the reason for all this hot action is about. The ingenue in this tale of pain and sorrow is Sally December, A K A Sally D, A K A the reason for this lowly story of mine.

(*Lights come up on* SALLY *December, an attractive but clearly tough college girl, and a much younger* DEWDROP *rolling in an old beat-up Cadillac.*)

DEWDROP: She's the babe at the wheel. That's me, five years earlier. A bit less nasty, a whole lot more clean.

RADIO (*V O*): To combat the sudden and dramatic rise of violent crime in Brooklyn, the mayor's office is enacting a sunset curfew for the entire borough of Kings County. Anyone found wandering the streets past sunset will immediately be detained for the duration of the evening. In a morning news conference, Mayor Pena had the following to say—

SALLY: Flip the switch, bitch. This tired shit is bugging me out.

DEWDROP: Maybe we should head home, Sal. It's almost dark—

SALLY: What? You scared of the dark or somethin'?

DEWDROP: No.

SALLY: Cause I'm not. I like the dark.

DEWDROP: Get off me, whore.

SALLY: Then what's wrong, love?

DEWDROP: The radio just said—

SALLY: Correction, bitch. Radios can't "say" anything.

DEWDROP: What?

SALLY: Radios. They are incapable of speech. They project noise. Transmit frequencies. Relay electromagnetic signals that our ears detect as sound. But they cannot speak. Speaking is an attribute that infers cognitive and sentient thought. Radios are not sentient so thusly speech is something still outside their realm of capability. By using the expression, "The radio just said", you personify the radio as something other than just a noise box and that, my oriental love-bot, is dumb as a motherfucker.

DEWDROP: Bitch, are you stoned?

SALLY: I'm just correcting. If you're gonna hang with me, yella girl, you gotsa speak proper.

DEWDROP: Whatevs.

SALLY: And secondly—

DEWDROP: Oh, there's a secondly?

SALLY: Of course there is, bitch.

And, secondly, do you really believe that anyone is gonna arrest us? Here? In Brooknam? For someone to get arrested, baby girl, someone has to be there to do the arresting. And do you happen to see any bacon bits sprinkled anywhere in this diverse salad bowl of Bushwick?

DEWDROP: Well...

SALLY: Now look hard. What does your eye spy?

DEWDROP: Nuthin'.

SALLY: Then shut your pretty little pie hole, cause you and me are on an adventure.

DEWDROP: For some pot?

SALLY: Well, when you say it that way, it doesn't make it sound special.

DEWDROP: Couldn't we have just scored some from the stoners down the hall?

SALLY: Ew no. I'm not going anywhere near those two midwestern motherfuckers. Have you seen the way they look at us?

DEWDROP: No.

SALLY: They'd want hand jobs.

DEWDROP: All guys want hand jobs.

SALLY: Well, if you wanna whore yourself for some hash, that is your prerogative. Me, I want my icky wicky coming from somewhere respectable.

DEWDROP: Like Bushwick?

SALLY: Yo, the only people that find Bushwick scary is white folks.

DEWDROP: Um. You're white.

SALLY: Just on the outside.

DEWDROP: Is there any other way of being white?

SALLY: Look, yella girl, underneath this blandy Mandy exterior is a girl of much more cultural charisma and street know-how than some cracka from Connecticut.

DEWDROP: You are a cracker from Connecticut.

SALLY: But underneath—

DEWDROP: You're a honky.

Sal, your family has two homes. One in Connecticut, the other in the fucking Hamptons. You spent every summer during your adolescence going to—what—tennis camp? And you're now attending one of the most expensive colleges in the nation without carrying a student loan. You're not just white—you're fucking glow-in-the-dark radioactive neon white. You're so white, standing next to you, I look like the night.

SALLY: Oh, but you're forgetting one thing. *(She stops the car and puts it in park.)*

DEWDROP: And what's that?

SALLY: I'm a big ol' dyke who loves fucking brown girls. *(She leans over and gives* DEWDROP *a big ol' meaningful kiss.)* I think that'll keep me from voting Republican anytime soon.

DEWDROP: *Touché.*

SALLY: Tell me a story, baby girl.

DEWDROP: Once upon a time, there were two girls. They fell in love. They were happy.

SALLY: How does the story end?

DEWDROP: They end up ruling the world.

SALLY: You tell the best stories.

DEWDROP: I know.

SALLY: *(Noticing the time)*

Hang tight now. I'll be right back.

DEWDROP: Be careful.

SALLY: Don't worry about me, love. I'm white afterall. We believe in health insurance.

(SALLY *shows* DEWDROP *a gun.*)

DEWDROP: Sal.

SALLY: Just keep the car warm for me, hot stuff.

(SALLY *leans in and kisses* DEWDROP. *She then exits the car.*)

(*Video sequence: From* SALLY's *point of view, we see her leave the car after kissing* DEWDROP. *She walks down a long dark alleyway. As she turns the corner, she sees the back of* BOSS 2K *lingering over a dead body. She turns to run, but runs face first into a gang of* LONG TOOTHS. *She pulls out her gun and fires, but to no avail. We see her run back to the car as she is pursued by gangmembers. She arrives back to the car as we see* DEWDROP *still waiting patiently.* SALLY *pounds on the car door window.*)

SALLY: Open the door! Open the fucking door! Now, Dewdrop, open the door! Please!

(*As* DEWDROP *frantically tries to open the door,* LONG TOOTHS *suddenly surround the car and rip* SALLY *away. As* DEWDROP *finally opens the door,* SALLY *and her attackers are mysteriously all gone. All that's left is a puddle of blood and a gun.*)

(*Fade to...*)

(DEWDROP *alone on stage.*)

DEWDROP: (*Addressing the audience*) Sally's was my Lady—the only girl I've ever dropped the L-bomb on. We were supposed to grow old together, she was supposed to be to my Queen, but instead five years ago she died in Kings County by the hands of the Long Tooths.

I wasn't strong enough to fight them then, but today,

it's an entirely different story.

(Cut to...)

(Lights come up on HURT, *one of Grandmaster Mack's gangstas, guarding the Brooklyn Bridge [the last and only bridge connecting Brooklyn to Manhattan]. He talks to* BURNOUT *who's offstage.)*

HURT: Yo, this shit is tired, G. I'm telling you we gotsa go find us a gig where we can meet some ladies cause this spot is dead.

BURNOUT: *(Entering the stage)* So what's the word?

HURT: Nuthin', G. Same shit as always.

BURNOUT: That's good.

HURT: A little action be nice.

BURNOUT: Fuck that. You know how long I been waiting for a gig like this? Shit, son, I useta have to smack hoes for Mack. This bent is nice.

HURT: Just boring is all.

BURNOUT: Yo, boring is better than having to work ballistics all the time.

HURT: Word.

BURNOUT: Better than having to do bounce work at some drug club. Shit, chigga, I'm just glad to be out of the action.

*(*DEWDROP *and* CERT *enter.)*

HURT: Yo, speaking of action...

DEWDROP: Stop following me, fool.

CERT: I ain't following you. We just happen to be going the same way, that's all. It's a coincidence.

DEWDROP: I'm gonna coincidentally kick you in your junk you don't break off.

BURNOUT: *(To* DEWDROP) Why, hello, hello. The fuck is

this?

HURT: What up, fine stuff?

BURNOUT: *(To* HURT*)* Yo, keep your tang cool, fool. *(To* DEWDROP*)* Where you think you going, Miss pigtails?

DEWDROP: The Badlands.

BURNOUT: Brooklyn?

DEWDROP: Did I stutter? You boys are in my way.

BURNOUT: Yo, pigtails. I don't know what you been tokin', but only F B A are allowed to cross this bridge.

DEWDROP: Who says I'm not?

*(*DEWDROP *pulls out a medallion and tosses it to* BURNOUT.*)*

CERT: Boo-yah.

DEWDROP: Shut up.

BURNOUT: Where the fuck you get this?

DEWDROP: The tooth fairy, bitch. Where do you think I got it?

BURNOUT: No way.

DEWDROP: Let me by.

BURNOUT: Yo, how do we know you didn't just forge this shit?
    This could be some counterfeit goods.

HURT: Yeah, counterfeit.

DEWDROP: Look, you two fucking douchebags, call up your Shogun, he'll give me the clear.

BURNOUT: You want us to call G-Mack?

DEWDROP: No. I want you to move out my muhfuckin' way, but if you got to call your pimp before you can move your ho ass, then do it.

BURNOUT: I don't like the way you're speaking to me.

DEWDROP: Well, I don't like yo' face. Now move before I gotta rain some pain on you motherfuckers.

CERT: Yeah, son, we will kick yo' ass.

BURNOUT: Who the fuck are you?

CERT: I'm—

BURNOUT: Fatboy.

HURT & BURNOUT: *(Taunting)* Fat-boy. Fat-fat-boy. Fat-boy. Fat-fat-boy. Fat-

CERT: HEY! The name's Cert. As in Death Cert...ificate.

(HURT & BURNOUT fall into hysterical laughter.)

CERT: Yo, why you laughin?

BURNOUT: Look, you two are cute and all, but we're F B A, bitch. You ain't got nuthin' on us.

HURT: Word.

BURNOUT: So why don't you turn that fine ass of yours around and swish the fuck outta here?

DEWDROP: I'm not going nowhere.

BURNOUT: Look, lady, I don't wanna do this by force. But... if I have to... I'm gonna make it fun for myself.

(BURNOUT steps towards DEWDROP.)

(DEWDROP drop kicks him to the ground.)

HURT: Oh no, she didn't!

BURNOUT: What the fuck?

HURT: Yo, G, you jus give me the what's up
and I'll fuck that bitch the fuck up.
I'm talkin' straight up messed up.
I'll be smackin' her sayin' "Whaddup!".

BURNOUT: Yo, back up. I got this.
Okay, bitch, you wanna play it that way. Let's play.

(BURNOUT pulls out a weapon.)

(DEWDROP *pulls out her sword.*)

(*They start towards each other.*)

(*Suddenly,* BURNOUT *grabs a handful of dirt and throws it in* DEWDROP*'s face. She's blinded.*)

BURNOUT: Oh, yeah, I like to play dirty.

(BURNOUT *and* HURT *begin doing a number on* DEWDROP. *Seeing enough,* CERT *intervenes and fights the gangsters. As it turns out, he's not that bad. He knocks out* BURNOUT *and* HURT.)

CERT: (*Fighting back tears*) That's right, muthafuckahs, that's my girl. That's MY GIRL you talking at. What's my name, what's my muhfuckin' name, bitch?

DEWDROP: When'd you learn all that, bozu?

CERT: (*Still fighting back tears*) What I could say? Imma badass, yo.

DEWDROP: Yeah, you one slick Rick right about now. And you skinny.

CERT: Yeah, it's just a style.

DEWDROP: Yeah.

CERT: I'm slick, smooth, and I smell good too.
So, yo, fly girl, can I come with you?

DEWDROP: Cert...

CERT: Seriously, that was some fly shit, you gotta admit. Come on, we make a good team. Yo, what are you gonna do the next time someone throws shit all up in your face?

(*Beat*)

DEWDROP: Fine. But if you fuckin' die, I'll fuckin' kill you myself.

CERT: That's my girl!

DEWDROP: Come on.

CERT: HELLO, BROOKLYN!!!

(A song like Jay-Z's Hello, Brooklyn 2.0 *begins playing as lights fade.)*

Two

(Projection: INTERLUDE ONE: THE COMPLETELY UNINTERESTING TALE OF MARCUS MOON*)*

(Lights come up on MARCUS *and an actor in neutral mask. The neutral mask actor [who will be referred to as* NEUTRAL MASK MARCUS*] is dressed exactly like* MARCUS *and physically acts out all the words that* MARCUS *says.)*

(Note: Though the following has markings that indicate a voiceover, these sections are not voiced over. It is only meant to mark when Marcus is directly addressing the audience or as a character in the scene.)

MARCUS: *(V O. Addressing the audience)* This was a typical day for me.

*(*NEUTRAL MASK MARCUS *staring into a bathroom mirror.)*

MARCUS: *(To* NEUTRAL MASK MARCUS*)* I am a worthwhile person and I'm going to make the world see me. I am a worthwhile person and I'm going to make the world see me. I am a worthwhile person and I'm going to make the world see me.
   Pathetic, isn't it? The truth is I'm not a worthwhile person. Not in the grand scheme of things. None of us are. Look around the room you're in, see the people sitting next to you. That person at the right of you is insignificant and that person at the left of you is insignificant. Let's be honest here, none of us are the next Mozart or Abraham Lincoln or Aristotle. We're all just pawns to be moved, ignored, and sometimes eaten. Actually, we're less than insignificant. We're scenery.

(Cut to...)

(NEUTRAL MASK MARCUS *standing in a subway car with tons of people crowded next to him.*)

MARCUS: *(V O)* Here's me amongst the sheep doing my best sardine impression. If the train crashed at this very moment, if we all died excruciating and painful deaths, we'd at least be close to something slightly memorable. We'd be the sad victims to some tragic tragedy that'd finally make it on the front page. To be remembered, it's all about death. Either die in some fantastic fashion or kill enough people that people want you dead. James Dean or Jeffrey Dalmer, it's all the same.

(Cut to...)

(NEUTRAL MASK MARCUS *at his desk.*)

MARCUS: *(V O)* This is a fairly common image. Look at me toil away at papers like it matters. Look at me try to be a useful part of society. And now watch me try to make the world finally see me.

ANGELA: Hey Marcus.

MARCUS: Hello, Angela.

ANGELA: Did you see the paper today? Three police precincts in Crown Heights, Brownsville, and Bed-Sty got blown up. It's getting scary out there, isn't it?

MARCUS: Yeah.

ANGELA: I think it may be time to move out of here. Brooklyn isn't safe anymore.

MARCUS: *(To himself)*

I am a worthwhile person and I will get the world to see me.

ANGELA: What was that?

MARCUS: Um, what are you up to this weekend?

ANGELA: This weekend?

MARCUS: Yes, because if you're not—

ANGELA: Oh my god, this weekend is crazy. I have
a date with this guy I met online. Online! Can you
believe it? I never saw myself as a person that would
do something like that, but you know how it is—it's
so hard to meet anyone anymore. Everyone's staying
indoors cause of all of the crime. My neighborhood bar
just went under because of it. How about you?

MARCUS: Um... I have some things to do.

ANGELA: Like what? Any hot dates?

MARCUS: Well, as you said...it's tough out there.

ANGELA: It is.

MARCUS: I hope you have a good time.

ANGELA: Thanks, Marcus. You're the best.

MARCUS: *(V O)* I will always wonder if things would
have been different if she bothered to see me. Maybe if
she would have noticed me as something worthwhile,
I would have believed it too. Maybe...if only...who
knows? Maybe I would have had something to do that
night instead of walking home with a bag full of rented
movies and a six pack of beer. Maybe...

(NEUTRAL MASK MARCUS *gets suckered punched by*
T-BONE. T-BONE *points a gun at* NEUTRAL MASK
MARCUS's *head.)*

T-BONE: Yo, *puta.* You scared?

MARCUS: Yes.

T-BONE: What, bitch? I didn't hear you!

MARCUS: YES. I'm scared.

T-BONE: How scared are you?

MARCUS: I'm not sure. How scared would you like to
be?

T-BONE: Is that supposed to be funny?

MARCUS: No. It's not. It's just...I just really want to make you happy.

T-BONE: You want to make me happy, *puta*?

MARCUS: Yes, sir.

T-BONE: Now I'm a sir?

MARCUS: Look. I have money, alright. You can have all of it.

T-BONE: Where?

MARCUS: In my wallet. Just take it.

T-BONE: See, this is what we call a good business transaction. A fair trade in services. I don't shoot you, you pay me...twelve dollars? You just got twelve fuckin' dollars, *pendajo*?

MARCUS: I'm sorry, I didn't know what was in there.

T-BONE: This is insulting, *pendajo*. When I'm insulted, I get twitchy. And a twitchy mutherfucker witha gun ain't so good for you, bro. You dig?

MARCUS: You can take my A T M card. I'll give you my pin.

T-BONE: You'll give me more than just your fuckin' pin.

MARCUS: What?

T-BONE: Give me your kicks.

MARCUS: My what?

T-BONE: Your shoes, *pendajo*. Your fuckin' shoes.

MARCUS: Okay.

T-BONE: Give me that jacket too.

MARCUS: Alright.

T-BONE: And—

MARCUS: I don't have anything else.

T-BONE: Your eyes.

MARCUS: What?

T-BONE: Your fucking eyes, *pendajo*. You see me, right?

MARCUS: Uh...

T-BONE: "Uh" is not a fucking word, bitch. You see me, right? And you hear me.

MARCUS: Yes.

T-BONE: Well, see. That's a problem. You see me. You hear me. Which means if you decide to get all describe-y to some pig about your friendly neighborhood "me" then I'm not gonna be able to see my momma no more. Now that's not a good story, is it?

MARCUS: I won't say a word. I swear.

T-BONE: Now how can we guarantee that?

MARCUS: I don't—

T-BONE: Don't worry, *pendajo*. I got an idea!

(T-BONE *shoots* NEUTRAL MASK MARCUS.)

(*The stage lights go dark except for a spotlight solely on* NEUTRAL MASK MARCUS. *We watch him slowly bleed out as the next monologue happens.*)

MARCUS: (*V O*) Dying is such a strange sensation. It's both extremely painful as well as uniquely relaxing. As the bullet violently rips its way into your body, the pain you feel is excruciating. As internal organs are damaged and destroyed, your body immediately goes into shock. With the pain, add in cold chills, shivering, and now, strangely, a sudden need to sleep. Yes, sleep. There's the rub. You want to writhe, but your body begins shutting down. Your eyes are heavy, your vision begins to blur, and your mind feels euphoric. It's better than any drug imaginable. You feel heaven tickling at your soul. But the hurt. The hurt, as dreadfully painful as it is, is now your only earthly friend. Hurt reminds us that we're still breathing, that we're still alive. Hurt reminds us that we're human. But "sleep", she is one sexy bitch and she will soon win.

LADY SNOWFLAKE: Wake up, hot stuff.

(Lights slowly come up revealing a masked LADY SNOWFLAKE, *a very hot assassin, sitting near the fallen* NEUTRAL MASK MARCUS. T-BONE *lies dead next to her.)*

MARCUS: What?

LADY SNOWFLAKE: I said wake up.

MARCUS: Are you... the grim reaper?

LADY SNOWFLAKE: What?

MARCUS: Are you death?

LADY SNOWFLAKE: Do I look like death?

MARCUS: Not exactly.

LADY SNOWFLAKE: You're not dead if that's what you're wondering. Not like him anyhow.

MARCUS: Who? Oh my god...

LADY SNOWFLAKE: Yeah, he's pretty fucked up. He's already bled out. That didn't take long.

MARCUS: Is he...

LADY SNOWFLAKE: Food for maggots? Yep, I'd say so.

MARCUS: He was going to kill me.

LADY SNOWFLAKE: Yeah, he was probably going to do alotta things. I'm sure he didn't think he'd end up faced down on some piss covered concrete when he woke up this morning. Life's pretty funny, huh?

MARCUS: Thank you.

LADY SNOWFLAKE: What?

MARCUS: Thank you.

LADY SNOWFLAKE: Why are you thanking me for?

MARCUS: For saving me.

LADY SNOWFLAKE: I didn't save you.

MARCUS: Then who did this?

LADY SNOWFLAKE: You're kidding, right?

MARCUS: About what?

LADY SNOWFLAKE: You really don't know?

MARCUS: Should I?

LADY SNOWFLAKE: Hot stuff, you did that to him.
You killed him.

MARCUS: I what?

LADY SNOWFLAKE: Yeah, as it turns out, you got some
skills. Who knew?

(NEUTRAL MASK MARCUS *slowly approaches and examines
the fallen* T-BONE.)

MARCUS: *(V O)* No, none of us are Mozart. None of us
are Aristotle. But that does not mean we don't all long
for immortality.

(In the Present tense)

(Cut to...)

DEWDROP: *(Addressing the audience)* After whacking
Boss 2K, Cert and I find ourselves inside a proverbial
Brooklyn fire. Trying to exterminate one pest, we
end up stirring up the whole hornets nest. Now all of
Kingsborough County is noisy with the bang clang
of bad guys out for blood for yours truly. We've been
fighting for over an hour straight and it doesn't seem
like the violence it gonna stop anytime soon. The
good news is we're no longer near the coast. The bad;
though we may no longer be smelling salt water, we're
still miles away from tasting home.

(Projection: The present)

(Projection: East Flatbush, Brooklyn)

(Lights come us as CERT *wanders the streets alone. Suddenly he gets attacks by a* LONG TOOTH. DEWDROP *saves him.)*

DEWDROP: Good job, Cert

CERT: Ninja, please. Next time, yo muhfuckin' ass is gonna play decoy. These bitches can hit.

(Cut to...)

(A bit later)

CERT: Yo, why these fuckahs still chasin' us anyways. I thought you said once we whacked their boss, they'd be getting the fuck outta dodge.

DEWDROP: Guess they didn't get the memo.

CERT: Yo, so what are we gonna do now?

DEWDROP: Get back to the Apple, that's what.

CERT: That's not what I mean. I mean "how". We can't just fight our way back home. Too many of 'em. Too little of us.

DEWDROP: Shhh!

(A LONG TOOTH *enters the stage.* CERT *suddenly emits a gasp which alerts the gangmember. He turns to attack,* DEWDROP *slays him.)*

DEWDROP: *(To* CERT*)* I don't think we got a better option than doing this kamikaze style.

(Cut to...)

(A bit later.)

CERT: Yo, hold up. Where we at?

DEWDROP: East Flatbush.

CERT: Yo, there's a subway station near here.

DEWDROP: A what?

CERT: A subway. As in the M T A.

DEWDROP: I know what a subway is.

CERT: We should go there.

DEWDROP: And what? We gonna wait there until some non-existent car is gonna come pick us up. For the subway to be useful, Cert, there needs to be subway cars. There hasn't been a working line in Brooklyn for years now.

CERT: I know that.

DEWDROP: Then why you wanna talk retard for?

CERT: I'm not retarded. I'm just sayin' the tunnels—

(CERT and DEWDROP get attacked again by LONG TOOTHS. They slay their attackers.)

DEWDROP: Yo, I ain't walking through no subway tunnels. That shit is suicide.

CERT: It's better than this. Out here we're walking dead—targets to get whacked. Underground, they can't see us.

DEWDROP: And we can't see them.

(Cut to...)

(Yet a bit later still.)

CERT: You really think any of them are hiding out in tunnels at night? It's the best option.

DEWDROP: I trust what I can see. And what I can see is a sword in my hand and this sword ain't much use if I can't see the muthafuckah I'm stickin' it with.

CERT: All I'm sayin' is we got flashlights and the tunnels provide... ow.

DEWDROP: You okay?

CERT: Muthafuckah got me good. Fucked me up like a snitch at a sock party.

DEWDROP: Let me look at you.

(DEWDROP *examines* CERT.)

CERT: It ain't nuthin. I still got my swing, yo.

DEWDROP: Cert. Your ribs look broken.

CERT: At least he didn't hurt my money maker. My face is still looking fine. You want up on this?

DEWDROP: This isn't time for jokes.

CERT: Who's joking?

DEWDROP: We gotta get you back to the Apple and quick.

CERT: There's no traffic on the subway line. Just sayin'.

DEWDROP: Cert.

CERT: I can't keep fighting like this, Dewdrop. We might be badass, but we ain't exactly Chuck Norris. I can hold my own, but how long before we walk into a swarm of those things, huh?

DEWDROP: Fine.

CERT: What?

DEWDROP: I said fine. Desperate times call for some... well, some suicidal measures.

CERT: Yeah, that's what I'm talking about!

(*He tries to high-five her. She leaves him hanging.*)

Three

(*Projection:* CHAPTER TWO: A DROP OF BLOOD ON THE BLADE MAKES IT SHINE)

(*During the next monologue, we see illustrations projected on the backwall depicting the evolution of the new N Y C.*)

DEWDROP: (*Addressing the audience*) Like myself, the N

Y C used to not always be such a rough and tumble place. But that was before the big war, before the great big three that tore up the country and left the city that never sleeps a carcass of its former self, before the ganglords took over and divided the five boroughs into dozens of neighborhood Fiefdoms held together solely by who could manage the most violence. In the end, three Shogun ruled the city—Grandmaster Mack of Manhattan, my former teacher Master Leroy Green of Queens, and the mysterious Boss 2K of Brooklyn.

Me, I wasn't always a killer. No one is born this way. That's not to say I didn't have an aptitude for it. I've always had a bit of a violent streak. I just wasn't always as smooth.

(Lights come up on DEWDROP *getting the shit beat out of her by* KANE. *She fights back the best she can.)*

KANE: Yo, dyke, I told you to stay the fuck away from here.

DEWDROP: My girl, Sally December, hadn't been dead for more than a month and I soon found myself sucking down empty promises and bad circumstances to fill the void. Any lady that let me, I used and abused and my rep was getting around.

KANE: Keep away from my sister. She ain't no fag. So keep your carpet munching ass away from my block or, next time, I'm gonna have to do much worse than this.

*(*KANE *hits her again. She spits blood in his face and smiles.)*

DEWDROP: You hit like a girl.

*(*KANE *drops her again.)*

KANE: What's that, ya fucking cunt? I didn't hear you over the sound of your ass hitting the floor. I hit like a what again? I hit like a what?

DEWDROP: Like a girl, asshole. Maybe I should think

about dating you instead.

KANE: You dykes must like it rough, huh?

DEWDROP: Absolutely.

(DEWDROP *hits* KANE *in his crotch, immediately bringing him down.*)

DEWDROP: Tell your bitch sister that it's over anyways. I don't like having to truck all the way to Astoria just to get some. Sides, she grows up to look anything like your mother, that's one crazy ugly bitch I don't want any part of.

(DEWDROP *gives him an extra kick to the face for good measure.*)

(DEWDROP *stumbles down the road to a bus stop. She collapses on the bench.*)

DEWDROP: After Sally's death, Brooklyn was soon overrun by Long Tooths and the Police became too scared to venture over to Kings County any longer. I was a wreck. I lost my lady and, yet, I kept seeing her wherever I went.

(*The ghost of* SALLY *enters...*)

SALLY: That was some harsh shit you just spat, bozu.

DEWDROP: What, bitch?

SALLY: The part about their mother. That was a bit uncalled for, don't you think?

DEWDROP: Why the fuck do you care?

SALLY: Just cause I'm dead, baby girl, don't mean I don't give a damn about how my lady sounds.

DEWDROP: Who cares what some Filipino bitch and her brother thinks of me?

SALLY: You're a Filipino bitch, baby.

DEWDROP: Yeah, fuck'em all.

SALLY: Can I sit here with you?

DEWDROP: Do I got a choice?

SALLY: Not really.

DEWDROP: Then why are you asking?

SALLY: Cause, baby girl. Questions are the first step in gaining knowledge. And, as they say, knowledge is half the battle.

DEWDROP: *Knowing* is half the battle. That's what they say.

SALLY: Alas, I may be wise in many ways, but I'll submit that your cartoon knowledge is vastly superior to my own.

DEWDROP: Yeah, that's right.

SALLY: Tell me a story, baby girl.

DEWDROP: Ain't no more stories to tell.

SALLY: No? Well then let me tell you one. Once upon a time, there were two girls. They fell in love. But one died and the other is now sitting here wishin' she were dead too.

DEWDROP: How does that one end?

SALLY: I don't know. You tell me. But I hope it ends happy.

DEWDROP: Yeah, I was a cliche' of self-inflicting pain. I was hurting and I wanted to hurt. I wanted revenge. I knew who to blame for all this—the Longtooths—but had no power in stopping them.

(Lights come up on CERT *as he jams out wearing headphones.)*

DEWDROP: *(V O)* And that's when I met him...

CERT: *(To himself)*
My name is Cert

I'm here to kick it
Don't step to me, boy,
Cause my shit is wicked
Ninja fly shit is how I be dealin' it
I'm a Samurai, son, so you best be feelin' it

Konichiwa, bozu,
Fuck you up old Schoo'
Knock out ya teeth like a Eastside Sifu

Remember these words
Remember my face
I'm the C-E-R-T.
This hood's my place.

DEWDROP: Hey! Will you shut the fuck up?

CERT: Why hello there, fly girl.

DEWDROP: No, you don't have to come over—

CERT: Yo, baby, did you clean your pants with Windex? Cause I can practically see myself in them.

DEWDROP: That was lame.

CERT: My name? Did you just ask me my name?

DEWDROP: No, I said "That was lame".

CERT: My name is Damon. But my homies call me Cert. \You can all me anything you want.

DEWDROP: Don't sit by me. Okay, now you're sitting by me. Great. You're completely ignoring—

CERT: What's yo' name?

DEWDROP: Fuck off.

CERT: Is that Russian?

DEWDROP: Look, bozu. You should probably go ahead and give up cause I ain't /interested.

CERT: I love Russian chicks.

DEWDROP: Do I look Russian?

CERT: Not traditionally. But I'm black and I ain't
exactly dark-complected, now am I? My mom's Jewish.
But I'm hung like a brotha if you know what I mean...

DEWDROP: No, I certainly don't.

CERT: You wanna go find a place we can go talk in
private like?

DEWDROP: Look, I like girls, okay?

CERT: So do I.

DEWDROP: No. I'm a lesbian.

CERT: Well, Cinderella was a bum before she got
transformed by her Fairy Godmother.

DEWDROP: Are you my Fairy Godmother now?

CERT: No, but I do got a magic stick! HEY-O!

DEWDROP: That was horrible.

CERT: But it made you crack a smile.

DEWDROP: You stupid.

CERT: I might be stupid, but I ain't the one waiting at a
bus stop that hasn't seen a bus in over a year. What?

DEWDROP: Touché.

CERT: So do you wanna—

DEWDROP: No.

CERT: Okay. Can I just get your—

DEWDROP: No.
    Look, we're not going to hang out, we're not gonna
make time, be buds, bump fists, or be homies, not even
in the most general sense. I don't like you, okay? This
is not going to or ever going to happen, ya dig?

CERT: We'll see.

DEWDROP: I first came to Queens to escape. Brooklyn
was too dangerous, Manhattan was ruled too rigidly

by Grandmaster Mack. Queens became the last refuge
for regs like me. This was all to the credit of my then
teacher, Master Leroy Green.

(Cut to...)

(Lights up on MASTER LEROY, *an African American martial
arts master who strangely speaks with a deep, yet noble,
Japanese accent and dresses like a Kung Fu movie extra.)*

MASTER LEROY: Get offa my step!

DEWDROP: No.

MASTER LEROY: Reave!

DEWDROP: No.

MASTER LEROY: Don't make me show you back of
hand. I willa hurting you very badly.

DEWDROP: I know you will.

MASTER LEROY: Then why so obstinate?

DEWDROP: I wanna train.

MASTER LEROY: I no teach no more.

DEWDROP: Master Leroy. I need to learn.

MASTER LEROY: What for?

DEWDROP: Revenge.

MASTER LEROY: You wanting revenge. You go buy gun.
Much faster.

DEWDROP: Guns don't work.

MASTER LEROY: I no teaching no more. You want that,
go learn from different teacher.

DEWDROP: It's against the Long Tooths.

MASTER LEROY: What you have against Wrong Tooth?

DEWDROP: They killed my girlfriend.

MASTER LEROY: You a gay?

DEWDROP: Yes.

MASTER LEROY: I don't care about your love life. I care about peace. My peace. And my peace requiring you to go away.

DEWDROP: My girlfriend was Sally December. I think you knew her quite well.

MASTER LEROY: Sally.

DEWDROP: She was a student of yours, correct?

MASTER LEROY: She was very bright girl. Angry, but very smart.

DEWDROP: The Longtooths killed her. I want revenge.

(MASTER LEROY *suddenly attacks* DEWDROP. *She blocks two moves, but gets knocked on her ass by the third.)*

MASTER LEROY: You have no skill.

DEWDROP: I know that.

MASTER LEROY: You block okay. Not good, but better than nothing.

DEWDROP: I did take a year and a half of Taekwondo.

MASTER LEROY: You took a year and a half of shit. You try to fight with skills like that, you die very fast.
   You want to learn?

DEWDROP: Yes.

MASTER LEROY: Take this.

(MASTER LEROY *tosses* DEWDROP *a towel.)*

DEWDROP: What? Do you want me to go wax something?

MASTER LEROY: No, stupid. I wanting you to clean dirt off of your face. Come inside. Training begins tomorrow morning.

(Cut to...)

(Training montage: DEWDROP *learns Kung Fu with* MASTER LEROY *to a song like "The Love you Save" by the Jackson Five.)*

(The other actors carry flags that will sweep across the stage to change the montages from scene to scene. What we see is the following in the following order.)

(1. MASTER LEROY *tells* DEWDROP *to attack him.)*

(2. DEWDROP *on the floor as* MASTER LEROY *shakes his head at her.)*

(3. DEWDROP *attacks* MASTER LEROY *again, he knocks her away with ease.)*

(4. CERT *trying to get* DEWDROP'S *attention on the street, she hits him in the gut and pushes him away.)*

(5. MASTER LEROY *tosses* DEWDROP *across the stage.)*

(6. CERT *dancing as he helps* DEWDROP *up to her feet. She smiles at him.)*

(7. MASTER LEROY *shows* DEWDROP *an armbar. He hurts.)*

(8. DEWDROP *showing* CERT *an armbar. It does not work. He tries it on her. It hurts.)*

(9. MASTER LEROY *attacking* DEWDROP, *she is still not good enough to stop his attack.)*

(10. CERT *doing a short dance routine.)*

(11. MASTER LEROY *doing a short kata.)*

(12. DEWDROP *trying to do a kick combination, but failing.)*

(13. CERT *finishing his dance routine.)*

(14. MASTER LEROY *showing* DEWDROP *the kata. She can't follow. He beats her.)*

(15. DEWDROP *successfully doing the dance routine with* CERT. *They celebrate.)*

(16. DEWDROP *attacks* MASTER LEROY. *She scores a punch on him the same way he scored a punch on her from segment*

9.)

(17. Master Leroy attacks Dewdrop, she stops him with an armbar. It hurts. He gets back up and bows to her in approval. She smiles.)

(18. MASTER LEROY, DEWDROP, & CERT do the short dance routine. MASTER LEROY sucks at it. CERT beats him jokingly. CERT goes to hug DEWDROP, she shakes her head at him. And then hugs him. End montage sequence as the song fades.)

(Cut to...)

(MASTER LEROY tosses DEWDROP a boken (a wooden samurai sword used for training).

MASTER LEROY: Attack me.

DEWDROP: Ain't you gonna grab a stick too?

MASTER LEROY: A true Samurai can fight without use of sword. He—

DEWDROP: Or she.

MASTER LEROY: Or she can cut even without the use of blade.

DEWDROP: Bullshit.

MASTER LEROY: You want to try?

(DEWDROP attacks MASTER LEROY. He avoids all of her attacks. And then easily passes her guard to knock her down.)

DEWDROP: Holy shit.

MASTER LEROY: How was I able to stop you?

DEWDROP: Cause you're fucking crazy?

MASTER LEROY: No, little Dewdrop. It is because I having no fear of death. I can look at it and see it for what it is, just another transformation. Because I'm not scared to die, I can face death itself without any

weapon in my hand and still be able to walk away
breathing. Do you understand?

DEWDROP: I trained for five years under Master Leroy
Green, preparing for my eventual fight into Brooklyn.
As the gangwars ravaged on, he took on more
students to protect his corner of Flushing, Queens. We
became his army and he became the third and final
Shogun. The only noble Shogun. He brought us peace.
However...gangsters do get greedy.

(Cut to...)

(Lights come up on MASTER LEROY *who is meditating.)*

(A masked LADY SNOWFLAKE *enters.)*

LADY SNOWFLAKE: So sorry, Sensei, but yo' show is
over.

MASTER LEROY: I knowing it was only a matter of time.
Your kind have no honor.

LADY SNOWFLAKE: That hurts, especially coming from
someone who's gonna be dead so soon.

*(*LADY SNOWFLAKE *attacks* MASTER LEROY. MASTER
LEROY *escapes her attacks unscathed. He grabs his sword
and they go at it. She fights incredibly well, though.
However, using a technique very much like the one*
MASTER LEROY *used to defend against* DEWDROP, LADY
SNOWFLAKE *disarms* MASTER LEROY.)*

MASTER LEROY: That technique. Where did you learn
that?

*(*LADY SNOWFLAKE *stabs* MASTER LEROY.)*

LADY SNOWFLAKE: Who's gots the glow now, bitch?

*(*DEWDROP *enters.)*

DEWDROP: Master Leroy! Oh GOD!

*(*DEWDROP *sees her fallen Master. She makes eye contact
with* LADY SNOWFLAKE.)*

MASTER LEROY: You. Who are you?
Fuckin' Longtooth.

(DEWDROP *picks up a weapon. Instead of attacking though,*
LADY SNOWFLAKE *just walks away.*)

MASTER LEROY: Dewdrop.

DEWDROP: Master Leroy!

MASTER LEROY: Don't go after...

DEWDROP: Master...

MASTER LEROY: You cannot win.

(MASTER LEROY *dies.*)

(*Fade to...*)

(DEWDROP *slowly leaves her fallen master and walks
towards his sword that's been hanging in his dojo. She pulls
the blade down as powerful music begins playing. She begins
to go into a kata with the blade that raises in intensity. In the
final moment of the katana,* DEWDROP *emits a loud yell. She
refocuses...*)

DEWDROP: Master, I promise I will kill them all...

Four

(*Projection:* INTERLUDE TWO: THE COMPLETELY
UNINTERESTING TALE OF MARCUS MOON)

MARCUS: *(V O)* I tried to return to my humdrum
life of bookkeeping and filing. I tried to ignore what
had happened the night before, but something had
triggered inside of me. I started noticing things...
hearing things...

(*Lights come up on* NEUTRAL MASK MARCUS *and*
AVORY, *his office manager, sitting at a restaurant as we
hear the sounds of police sirens and gunshots happening
outside. As they talk, the sounds continue to grow until it's*

overwhelming...)

AVORY: Thanks for letting me take you out, Marcus.
I just wanted to let you know that you're doing an
incredible job. An incredible job. So thoroughly
incredible.

MARCUS: Thank you.

AVORY: I'm serious, Marcus, there's been very few
employees I'd be willing to say were as at the top of
their game as you, but you, my friend, are at the top of
your game.

MARCUS: Thanks. Do you hear anything?

AVORY: Hear what?

MARCUS: Alarms, gunshots...

AVORY: It's Brooklyn on a Tuesday night, what else do
you expect?

MARCUS: No, but it's just particularly loud tonight.

AVORY: Well, that's actually what I've brought you out
for. I'd like to talk to you about work. The heads of
the company have been discussing this for quite some
time.

MARCUS: Avory, that doesn't seem super loud to you?

AVORY: And, well, there's no real easy way of saying
this, but effective next month, we will be moving the
company out of New York.

MARCUS: Jesus.

AVORY: Yeah, I was shocked too when I heard, but
New York is going south really really fast. It's just not
smart to stay here anymore. The market can't sustain.

MARCUS: I can't fucking stand it.

AVORY: Me neither. N Y C just isn't what it used to be.

MARCUS: Goddamn it.

AVORY: Oh, but don't misunderstand, this is not what
you think. We're not laying you off. We want you to
come with us. That's why I brought you out. To offer
you your position in our new home out in Stamford,
Connecticut.

MARCUS: Shut up.

AVORY: No, I'm serious. Isn't that great—

MARCUS: Shut up.

AVORY: Marcus.

MARCUS: SHUT UP!

(NEUTRAL MASK MARCUS *grabs his knife and stabs* AVORY
in the chest. Everything goes quiet.)

AVORY: Marcus... why'd you do that?

(AVORY *dies.* MARCUS *gets up and runs away. We see him
run down the street.*)

MARCUS: *(V O)* I didn't know what was happening.
It was like my body just needed to see blood. And
Avory, his long talking incessant voice was tearing at
my braincells. I ran. I ran for blocks. And then, I ran
straight into her. The lady from last night.

LADY SNOWFLAKE: Curious what's happening to you?

MARCUS: You!

LADY SNOWFLAKE: It's nothing to worry about.
You're just remembering, that's all.

MARCUS: I killed another man.

LADY SNOWFLAKE: Good.

MARCUS: The fuck is happening to me?

LADY SNOWFLAKE: I told you. You're—

MARCUS: I'm not remembering shit. I'm just hearing
things.

LADY SNOWFLAKE: It's your body, Mister Moon. It's remembering what it is.

MARCUS: What it is? What are you, some kinda freaky new age witch? What it is? It's my body—that's what it is.

LADY SNOWFLAKE: You're remembering who you are. Your true self.

MARCUS: Look, ya gotta help me here.

LADY SNOWFLAKE: You don't need help, Mister Moon. You need to remember.

MARCUS: Remember what?

LADY SNOWFLAKE: Your real persona. The real person inside you. You're strong. Much stronger than you realize.

MARCUS: You're fucking crazy.

LADY SNOWFLAKE: Am I?

MARCUS: Why are you here?

LADY SNOWFLAKE: Cause you need to see.

MARCUS: See what?

(ANGELA and ONLINE enter, flirtatiously taunting the other.)

(From this point forward, NEUTRAL MASK MARCUS stands next to LADY SNOWFLAKE as MARCUS acts everything out himself.)

ONLINE: Come on, baby, let me come up. I know I ain't Fred Flintstone, but I do know I can make your bed rock.

ANGELA: Get off me.

ONLINE: Oh, I'd love to get off.

ANGELA: No, you drunk fuck. I mean ease off the throttle.

ONLINE: You don't want that.

ANGELA: Yes, I do.

MARCUS: Angela?

ANGELA: Stop.

ONLINE: Come here for a second.

ANGELA: Let go.

ONLINE: You're drunk.

ANGELA: Stop it!

MARCUS: ANGELA!

ANGELA: Marcus?

MARCUS: Are you okay?

ONLINE: Hey asshole, can't you see we're in the middle of something here? Why don't you mind your own fuckin' business?

MARCUS: Why don't you?

(MARCUS *reaches out and rips out* ONLINE'S *throat.*)

MARCUS: Angela, are you okay?

ANGELA: Oh my God.

MARCUS: Angela?

ANGELA: You... you just... oh god.

MARCUS: Angela, calm down.

ANGELA: You just killed him.

MARCUS: He was attacking you.

ANGELA: No, he wasn't.

MARCUS: You said help.

ANGELA: No, I didn't.

MARCUS: Yes, yes, you did.

ANGELA: No, I didn't. And how would you know?

MARCUS: I saw you.

ANGELA: You were spying on me?

MARCUS: No, I was just running and—

ANGELA: And what? You just showed up here on my step?

MARCUS: Yeah? I guess.

ANGELA: Stay away from me, creep.

MARCUS: Angie.

ANGELA: Don't touch me.

MARCUS: Angie, please.

I'm not trying to hurt you.

ANGELA: Stop it.

(ANGELA *grabs* MARCUS's *face and scratches him.*)

MARCUS: Why'd you do that?

ANGELA: I told you to let me go.

MARCUS: You hurt me.

ANGELA: Go home, Marcus.

MARCUS: You hurt me.

ANGELA: Marcus?

MARCUS: No one hurts me.

(MARCUS *jumps onto* ANGELA *and bites into her. His eyes have changed colors and his teeth have grown feral. As he feeds,* LADY SNOWFLAKE *sits beside him and talks.*)

LADY SNOWFLAKE: You're a Long Tooth, Marcus. The baddest kind of mofo this city's ever known.

(MARCUS *breaks away, afraid.*)

MARCUS: Who are you? Why are you here?

LADY SNOWFLAKE: You sent me here, baby. You're my boss afterall. You made me.

MARCUS: What?

LADY SNOWFLAKE: Your name, Marcus. Your real name is Prince Mamuwalde. You've had many in your long ass life. Some unforgettable, some regrettable, and one in particular made your legend laughable. But the truth is... you're much bigger than some name, baby. You're Boss 2K, the Kingsborough King, and you don't have to wear this mask no more. And with the world done gone asunder, it is your time to shine.

(As LADY SNOWFLAKE *finishes her speech,* MARCUS *has converted fully into* BOSS 2K. *He takes her by the hand.*)

MARCUS/BOSS 2K: Lady Snowflake. Let's go make some war.

Five

(*Projection:* CHAPTER THREE: NOT ALL THINGS BURIED STAY DEAD)

(*Cut to...*)

(Projection: Present.

(*Projection: Prospect Park Subway Station*)

(DEWDROP *and* CERT *run into an old abandoned subway car for shelter as we see* LONG TOOTHS *run by the window. One suddenly stops and looks into the car window [we see his eyes and teeth are not human]. As he peers, we see our heroes hiding below frightened. He is about to enter right when he hears the scream of a different Long Tooth. He runs after it.*)

CERT: Goddamn they are some fast muthafuckers.

DEWDROP: Well, it's not like they have to stop to catch their breaths.

How you holding up?

CERT: Could be worse. Could be dead.

(DEWDROP *checks to see if they're clear.*)

DEWDROP: They're gone.
Okay, you ready to do this?

CERT: Hell yeah.

DEWDROP: Flashlights.

CERT: Check.

DEWDROP: Sweet. Let's roll. Quietly.

(DEWDROP *and* CERT *run out of the subway car down into the subway tunnel.*)

(*A moment passes.*)

(CERT *runs back onto stage.*)

CERT: Yo, hold up.

DEWDROP: What is it?

CERT: Um, that tunnel is really fuckin' dark.

DEWDROP: No shit. It's a subway tunnel.

CERT: But it's really fuckin' dark. I didn't know shit could get that dark.

DEWDROP: What? You scared of the dark or somethin?

CERT: Um... no.

DEWDROP: Cert, this was your idea.

CERT: Yo, I didn't know it was going to be like that. It's just a bit—you know...

DEWDROP: Scary?

CERT: Yo, I ain't scared. You're scared. I'm just being cautious. I'm a cautious muthafuckah, you dig?
Remember, I actually used to live in Brooklyn. You don't pull off living in Brooklyn if you ain't got a big pair of—

DEWDROP: Do you want me to hold your hand?

CERT: Yes, please.

DEWDROP: Come on.

(DEWDROP *and* CERT *exit.)*

(Cut to...)

(Projection: MEANWHILE IN THE L E S)

(GRANDMASTER MACK *gets tossed onto the stage as* LADY SNOWFLAKE *walks towards him.)*

LADY SNOWFLAKE: Naughty naughty, you broke the rule.

GRANDMASTER MACK: The fuck you doing up in my crib, suckaaaah?

LADY SNOWFLAKE: There's a coupla bustas sporting black in the badlands. We had a deal.

GRANDMASTER MACK: No, baby, I had a deal with yo' Boss. Not you. If he gots beef, he can talk to me himself. I don't take spit from no one's bitch.

LADY SNOWFLAKE: Oh, I think you should reconsider that sentence, hot stuff.

GRANDMASTER MACK: Baby, I've seen yaiba's my whole life. No pokey stick is gonna scare me.

LADY SNOWFLAKE: Who said I was gonna kill you with this?

(GRANDMASTER MACK *attacks* SNOWFLAKE *with his pimp cane. He's clearly a very skilled fighter and gangboss.)*

(But SNOWFLAKE'S *even better. Right when she looks like she's about to lose the fight, she latches onto* GRANDMASTER MACK *and bites him.)*

GRANDMASTER MACK: *(As he is dying)* Aaaagh! White. Devil. Bitch.

(She kills him dead. As she finishes, she releases a very satisfied moan.)

LADY SNOWFLAKE: You regs are just too easy.

(Cut to...)

(DEWDROP and CERT walking through a dark subway tunnel. All we see is the light from their flashlights.)

CERT: Yo, what the fuck was that!?!

DEWDROP: Fool, get off me.

CERT: You know what, Dewdrop. Maybe this shit was dumb afterall...

DEWDROP: It's a little too late to turn back now.

CERT: This was a much better idea before I realized how fuckin' dark it is down here. I can't see shit. It's like trying to see through Tito Jackson's afro. Shit is black.

DEWDROP: Come on, Cert. The faster we get moving, the quicker we get out from underground.

CERT: OH FUCK!

DEWDROP: What?

CERT: Something just ran across my foot.

DEWDROP: It was prolly a rat.

CERT: A rat? Yo, there's fuckin' rats down here?

DEWDROP: Chigga, it is a subway.

CERT: Yo, you do know rats carry rabies.

DEWDROP: Oh fuck, you're right. Rabies. That's something we should really worry about right now. Considering we're underground, there's a city full of Long Tooths above us, and—

CERT: Ow!

DEWDROP: You're limping along with a broken rib. Yep. Those rabid rats are really an immediate danger right about now. What will we ever do?

CERT: You don't need to be sarcastic.

DEWDROP: Well then stop being stupid and just come on.

CERT: Yo, that's mean.

DEWDROP: I'm not being mean.

CERT: You just called me stupid.

DEWDROP: No, I said stop being stupid. There's a difference. One is a judgement call on you and the other is a critique of the stupid shit you're doing.

CERT: You do know I came here to help you, right? To protect you. There's no reason you gotta spit hate at me all the time.

DEWDROP: Cert.

CERT: Yo' ass can just be fuckin' cold sometimes.

DEWDROP: Look, I'm sorry, okay?

CERT: What?

DEWDROP: I said—

CERT: No, shut up.

DEWDROP: Yeah, that's really polite of you. /I mean I go out of my way to—

CERT: Shhhhhhhhhhhhh.

DEWDROP: What?

CERT: I thought I heard something.

DEWDROP: Like what? Another bloodthirsty rat?

CERT: No. Something else. It actually sorta sounded like—AAAAAH!

(CERT get's pulled into the darkness. His flashlight is out.)

DEWDROP: Cert? Cert! Yo, this shit isn't funny! Cert! You okay?

(As DEWDROP fans her flashlight around to find CERT, it

flashes pass an ominous hooded figure.)

DEWDROP: Oh shit.

(DEWDROP *suddenly gets attacked. She tries to fight the best she can. We only see glimpses of the struggle as the flashlight flashes on and off the action. She is surrounded and outnumbered.)*

(*Suddenly we hear a hard thunk and then darkness.)*

(*Three flashlights turn on pointed to the ground. There, we see the bodies of* CERT *and* DEWDROP *lying unconscious.)*

END OF ACT ONE

ACT TWO

One

(*Projection:* CHAPTER FOUR: IT NOW ONLY SNOWS
AT NIGHT...)

(*Projection: Brownsville Church of the Savior, Brooklyn)*

(*Lights come up on* DEWDROP *and* CERT *waking up on the
floors of a church. The* PASTOR, *a scarred and weathered
general of a man [sporting an eye-patch], is going over plans
with his troops [the hooded figures we met on the subway
tracks]. It is obvious the* PASTOR *has spent many years
fighting off the* LONG TOOTHS.)

PASTOR: (*Noticing the awake* DEWDROP *&* CERT) You two
young fools ain't from around these parts, are ya?

DEWDROP: How'd ya guess? Is it our hair?

PASTOR: Your friend looks much better now that he's
been bandaged up.

DEWDROP: What is this place?

PASTOR: Is it not obvious? It's a church, little Samurai.
I'm the Pastor of this parish. The ones that brought you
here were my congregation.

DEWDROP: That was your congregation?

PASTOR: What can I say? They're a lively bunch.

DEWDROP: So you're another Shogun, is that it?

PASTOR: No. I'm a preacher, young lady.

DEWDROP: I didn't know preachers carried weapons.

PASTOR: I guess you never heard of the crusades?

DEWDROP: Oh, I have. And as I recall, the crusades were a monumental disaster of historical proportions.

PASTOR: There's no shame in doing God's work.

DEWDROP: Right.

CERT: Yo, can we hold up in here until morning?

PASTOR: If you like.

DEWDROP: We're not staying here.

CERT: What? Why?

DEWDROP: We're in the heart of Brownsville. This place is swimming with Long Tooths. How long do you think it's gonna be before they pick up our scent.

PASTOR: I assure you this church is completely safe. We're well armed, well organized, and well in the eyes of God. Trust me, they are just as afraid of us as we are of them.

DEWDROP: I highly doubt that.

PASTOR: We, my dear girl, have the holy power of the cross protectin' us. They can't come in here.

DEWDROP: You're kidding me, right?

PASTOR: I would never kid about matters concerning God.

DEWDROP: Look, Father, forget what you heard. Long Tooths ain't afraid of that cross anymore than they are of garlic or mirrors. We done seen them first hand, they're hard to kill and even harder if the only thing you got protecting you is a wooden stick and a bucket full of Jesus. This church ain't safe.

PASTOR: You really believe that?

DEWDROP: As much as you believe that thing around your neck is gonna stop a hungry Long Tooth.
  Come on, Cert. It's time to go.

PASTOR: You may think our ways are foolish, little Samurai, but I don't think there's anything more foolish than walking these streets at night.

DEWDROP: Well, it's not like we got a better choice.

PASTOR: Again. You have no faith.

(PASTOR *tosses* DEWDROP *a set of keys.*)

DEWDROP: What's this?

PASTOR: Keys to our car.

CERT: Yo, you got a working car?

PASTOR: It's better than trying to walk, now isn't it?

DEWDROP: You're giving us your car?

PASTOR: A good samaritan does what he can. But I guess I'm not that because as you said... I'm a shogun.

CERT: This whack ass mofo is giving us his ride?

DEWDROP: If you got a car, how come you ain't using it?

PASTOR: What would I use it for?

DEWDROP: To get the fuck out of here, that's what.

PASTOR: Why would I want to do something as foolhardy as that?

CERT: Yo, you do know this is Long Tooth territory, right?

PASTOR: We've always had gang problems here. This is no different.

DEWDROP: The Long Tooths ain't just a gang, Preacher.

PASTOR: We know what they are.

DEWDROP: Then no offence, Pastor man. But are y'all fuckin' crazy?

PASTOR: Let me ask you something. Do you understand what the purpose of your life is?

DEWDROP: Yo, don't drop none of that Bible bullshit on me. I'm trying to help you here.

PASTOR: Do you understand your purpose?

(DEWDROP *says nothing.*)

PASTOR: Well, we do.

DEWDROP: Why? Cause you got God?

PASTOR: Look at my people. Do you know who they once were? These children bearing weapons and stakes. These warriors of God? These used to be the most feared and hated drug slinging slingers in all of the Brownsville. They used to destroy this neighborhood and now they fight to preserve it. For the first time in my life, we are unified. That, to me, is something worth fighting for. Before the Long Tooths, we were killing one another. And now –

DEWDROP: The Long Tooths are killing you.

PASTOR: Bottom line, little Samurai, this is our home. And we don't plan on leaving it.

CERT: Yo, these fuckahs are batshit.

PASTOR: I guess I shouldn't expect someone like you to understand.

DEWDROP: Someone like me?

PASTOR: Someone without any faith.

DEWDROP: Faith? Fuck that. I got something better. I got a sword.

PASTOR: And how long do you think you can go on with that?

DEWDROP: It's done us pretty good so far. Ain't that right, Cert?

CERT: Yeah, son.

DEWDROP: We whacked Boss 2K with it.

CERT: Sent that fuckah to his grave.

PASTOR: You did what?

DEWDROP: We may be "foolish", but we done saved you and all your borough. You're welcome.

PASTOR: You killed Boss 2K?

CERT: That's right.

PASTOR: You two are fools.

DEWDROP: Um, that's when you were supposed to say "thank you".

PASTOR: Do you really believe killing one man is going to stop an army?

DEWDROP: They're Long Tooths. You kill their boss and—

PASTOR: And what?

DEWDROP: And they go away, right?

PASTOR: This isn't a fairy tale, children. You can't just beat them with one fight.

(LADY SNOWFLAKE *suddenly enters.*)

LADY SNOWFLAKE: Hey, lunchmeat! Catch!

(*And* LADY SNOWFLAKE *throws a knife across stage that impales the* PASTOR *in his good eye. He falls dead.*)

LADY SNOWFLAKE: All that God talk really burns my soul. Don't you agree?

DEWDROP: You.

LADY SNOWFLAKE: Hello, love.

DEWDROP: You're the one who killed my sensei.

LADY SNOWFLAKE: Don't you mean "our sensei", baby doll?

DEWDROP: What?

CERT: Who the fuck is this white bitch?

(LADY SNOWFLAKE *removes her mask.*)

DEWDROP: Sally?

CERT: She's a Long Tooth!

LADY SNOWFLAKE: Come here and let me give you a big ol' kiss.

(DEWDROP *pulls out her sword.*)

DEWDROP: Cert. Run!

(*They run away.*)

Two

(*Projection:* INTERLUDE THREE: A BRIEF STORY ABOUT SNOWFLAKES)

DEWDROP: (*Like a Children's story*)
And now, the story of Lady Snowflake...
Once upon a time ago in a suburb far far away, there once was a little girl named Sally December. She was a pretty girl that wore thick rimmed specs and politically charged t'shirts. And though she grew up in an age of hipsters, scenesters, and wannebes, not an ounce of irony existed in her generous and genuine demeanor.

STRANGER: (*Played by a puppet*) Yo taxi!

SALLY: A moment for Democracy?

STRANGER: Fuck you.

SALLY: Are you a registered voter here in the state of New York?

STRANGER: Eat shit.

SALLY: Can I talk to you a bit about the future of America?

STRANGER: Shut the fuck up!

DEWDROP: The world didn't appreciate the young Sally December.

(A "World puppet" appears and acts out the next section.)

DEWDROP: Nice people like her didn't make sense in a place like the N Y C. With a broken economy and an unending war eating away at its soul, the world wad getting bleak and didn't need smiles coming from some strange outsider. So she did what any young happy girl does when the world gets too rough, she went to college. And there she hid as the world that didn't want her got darker and fell into even more disarray. But unlike the other college kids around her, she still heard the world's cries. She still felt its pain and did the only thing she could do to make it all better. She drank the drink of the disenchanted.

SALLY: Fuck these mothefuckers. Fuck'em all. Fuck you, world. You got me? I ain't loving you no more!

DEWDROP: *(V O)* So Sally December drank more of the drink of disenchantment.

And one day as she wandered the streets ignoring the people she once tried to help, she came upon a house far from her college campus, far from her broken home of the East Village, she found herself at the doorsteps of the wise Master Green.

(Though previously MASTER LEROY was played by a real actor, in this section of the play, MASTER LEROY is performed by a puppet that exactly resembles the actor.)

MASTER LEROY: Get offa my step!

SALLY: Fuck you, old man. I'm gonna sit where I wanna sit. It's a free country.

MASTER LEROY: Young lady, are you crazy?

SALLY: Fuck you!

MASTER LEROY: Young lady?

DEWDROP: Seeing how lost she was, the Master took in Sally December and tried to nurse her back to health the best he could. He shared with her all he had—his food, his home, and his secrets.

MASTER LEROY: You cannot give up on the world, Sally. When the world is most dark, that is when we must be our most brightest. When the world cannot hear us, we must screaming louder. When the it cannot see us, we must become bigger. Do you understand?

SALLY: You want me to get fat?

MASTER LEROY: No, Sally. I wanting you to fight.

SALLY: Seriously, Master Leroy, what can I do? I'm just one girl.

MASTER LEROY: That is why you needing to find new friend. A partner who can helping you stand up strong. Someone you can love.

DEWDROP: (V O) Little Sally December listened to her teacher's words closely. And she took those words to heart and returned to the world that didn't want her. And she began her battle anew.

STRANGER: Yo taxi!

SALLY: Did you hear this? Mayor Pena is cutting down funding for police in Brooklyn. They're taking cops off the street. Are we gonna stand for this?

STRANGER: Fuck you.

SALLY: No, fuck you, motherfucker.

STRANGER: What?

SALLY: You heard me. I said fuck you. You don't wanna give a shit about what happens in your fuckin'

hood, then go move to somewhere else. This is my city
and I actually give a shit.

STRANGER: Yo, bitch, take a chill pill.

SALLY: What did you say to me?

STRANGER: I said take a fuckin' chill pill. This is
Manhattan. Who gives a shit about Brooklyn anyways.
I'm glad you like handing out flyers, but flyers ain't
changing shit. There's a world out there you don't
understand, white girl. A world you ain't never gonna
understand.

(The words "Never understand" echoe as the STRANGER
puppet flips off SALLY.)

DEWDROP: "Never understand?" Sally December did
not like these words at all, but down deep she knew
they were true. She had grown up like a princess
with a silver spoon in one hand and white privilege
in the other. So she did what any good happy young
girl would do, she studied and learned and found a
new hiding place inside the confines of libraries and
wikipedia sites to fill her mind and let her learn all
about a world she never understood.

SALLY: Yo, you got anymore books on these cats, the
Mamuwalde family?

DEWDROP: The what?

SALLY: The Mamuwalde family.

DEWDROP: That's a funny name.

SALLY: Yeah, whatevs.

DEWDROP: Let me check.

SALLY: Thanks.

DEWDROP: Hey, aren't you that girl who's always
screaming all the time out in the quad.

SALLY: What about it?

DEWDROP: I'm just making an observation.

SALLY: An observation, huh?

DEWDROP: Yeah.

SALLY: Oh come on, you can tell me what you think. I done heard it all. "Fuck you, bitch. Eat shit. Go fuck yourself."

DEWDROP: I wasn't going to say that.

SALLY: Oh, you weren't, were you? You got another creative way of telling me I'm a fuckin' nutjob?

DEWDROP: No, I was gonna tell you that it's really courageous when people say the things that they think and that you do that and that I think that it's really awe... some.

SALLY: Oh yeah?

DEWDROP: It's cool to see you do it. I could never.

SALLY: And why's that?

DEWDROP: Note the Asian exterior. Asian people, as you may or may not know, are infamous about being the quiet type. I don't think I could ever be so loud.

SALLY: Oh, I don't know. I think I could help you get pretty loud if that's what you wanted.

DEWDROP: Oh, would you now?

SALLY: Sorry, that's not what I mean.

DEWDROP: It's okay if it was.

SALLY: Oh?

DEWDROP: My name's Dewdrop, by the way.

SALLY: Sally December.

DEWDROP: That's a funny name, Sally December.

SALLY: Oh, and Dewdrop is just the most common one in the book.

DEWDROP: Okay, you got a point.
It's nice to meet you, Sally December.

SALLY: Same here, hot stuff. Same here.

DEWDROP: And just like that, the world that didn't
want Sally December still didn't want her, but she no
longer was bothered by the fact. Because now, she had
a partner. Someone that made the world seem not so
dark at all. *(To* SALLY*)* Are you still reading?

SALLY: What? I like to read.

DEWDROP: Come here.

SALLY: Why?

DEWDROP: Dance with me.

SALLY: You're a dork.

DEWDROP: Come on.

SALLY: You want me to dance with you, baby girl?

DEWDROP: Always.

(SALLY *and* DEWDROP *begin slow dancing.)*

(Lights fade to black.)

Three

(Projection: The Brooklyn/Queens Expressway, Brooklyn.)

(Lights come up on CERT *and* DEWDROP *driving in a
Honda Civic. Behind them is an 18-wheeler filled with Long
Tooths.)*

DEWDROP: I'm speeding across the the Brooklyn/
Queens Expressway as my ex-girlfriend's gangsters
are hot on my trail. I'm weaving between broken down
heaps, hoping beyond hope I don't slam face first
into a roadblock of broken down rides. Those Long
Tooths, however, are rolling Madmax style with an

18 wheeler slamming through abandoned S U Vs and hybids. Where I gotta swerve, they're steady, knocking through debris like they were dominos. Shortest distance between two points is a straight line. That being the case—

CERT: Holy shit, they're gaining on us!

DEWDROP: Cert is pissin' his pants. Literally. The stench nearly makes me lose my balance. I tell him to grab the wheel.

CERT: What?

DEWDROP: Grab the muthafuckin' wheel, mutherfucker. I'm gonna go do me some killin'.

CERT: How you gonna do that?

DEWDROP: I slide out the sunroof. The 18-wheeler is now literally kissing the ass of our small, yet gas efficient Honda Civie. As it tries to bumper car us off the road, I take a leap of faith and now I'm hanging on the 18-wheeler's grill. I fight to climb up onto the hood as the driver signals for his boys to take me out. They hesitantly follow his orders, but I kill'em as soon as they rear their heads. I crash my sword through the windshield of the 18-wheeler. It kills the driver instantly. We crash. I fall.

(DEWDROP passes out. SALLY enters.)

SALLY: Wake up, baby girl.

DEWDROP: Sally?

SALLY: Tell me a story...

DEWDROP: Stay away from me!

SALLY: Worry not, love, I'm just a figment. Not real in the least bit.

DEWDROP: You're not?

SALLY: Am I biting your neck right now?

DEWDROP: You're a fuckin' Long Tooth.

SALLY: Yeah, ain't that a somethin?

DEWDROP: How is that possible?

SALLY: Come on, baby girl, you know. Sometimes when a Longtooth meets a Reg, and they really dig on each other, sometimes they get the inclination to get sorta necky. And when that happens—

DEWDROP: You're joking.

SALLY: No, I'm stating an obvious, my Oriental love-bot. I'm being Capitano Obvious-O. There's a difference.

So now what are you going to do, baby girl?

DEWDROP: I want to go home.

SALLY: That's it?

DEWDROP: That's all I can do.

SALLY: What about me?

DEWDROP: What about you?

SALLY: I thought you promised you'd "Kill them all". For your teacher. For your lover. For Brooklyn.

DEWDROP: The circumstance has changed.

SALLY: You're quite the hero.

DEWDROP: What do you want from me?

SALLY: I want you to tell me a story.

DEWDROP: What story?

SALLY: Once upon a time, there were two girls. One who promised to kill all the monsters and one who became a monster herself. How does it end?

DEWDROP: I don't know.

SALLY: It's simple. Either the monster dies or the hero does. Your call.

DEWDROP: I can't kill you.

SALLY: You can't?

DEWDROP: I won't.

SALLY: Then, baby girl, I think you're in quite a predicament. Cause I'm pretty sure that I'm not gonna have the same prob ripping out your pretty little heart the next time I see you. Especially now that you got no sword, no sidekick, and with that limp holding you back, definitely no style. I'd say you're officially in a world of suck.

DEWDROP: I'll be fine.

SALLY: Will you? Cause, baby, I might not know alotta shit, but I do know one thing.

DEWDROP: What's that?

SALLY: I know you should probably turn the fuck around right about now.

DEWDROP: Why?

(*As* DEWDROP *turns*, BOSS 2K *appears and slugs* DEWDROP. *She flies across the stage from the impact.*)

BOSS 2K: Uh oh, looks like someone forgot to kill somebody all the way.

Hold still, Mama. This is just gonna hurt a little. But, don't worry, it's the good kinda hurt.

DEWDROP: No, stop. Please! Please!

(*As he's about to bite into her,* CERT *jumps in and kicks him off* DEWDROP.)

CERT: Surprise, bitch! Remember me!

(CERT *and* BOSS 2K *go at it one on one. The fight goes back and forth, but* CERT *finally wins when he busts out fight moves that resemble his b-boy dance steps.*)

CERT: Boo-yah! I told you that you would need me.

DEWDROP: Cert!

You came back for me.

CERT: You're my girl, ain't ya? I ain't gonna let anything happen to my girl. Even if she won't let anything happen between us.

DEWDROP: I'm not gonna lie—you are making it tempting right about now.

CERT: What can I say? My game is too tight.
  Now cut off that muthafuckah's head, will ya?

DEWDROP: What?

CERT: I said cut off that muthafuckah's head. You're my sidekick, ain't ya? That's yo' job.

DEWDROP: I guess it is.

BOSS 2K: Except one small problem, suckah. I ain't dead yet!

(BOSS 2K leaps up and bites CERT. CERT impales and kills BOSS 2K.)

CERT: Sayonara, Muthafuckaaaaaaaaaaaaaa! Hehehe. Oh fuck, I don't feel so good. *(He falls.)*

DEWDROP: Cert!

CERT: I think he got me.

DEWDROP: Goddammit! Why didn't you just drive back to the Apple?

CERT: Cause you'd be dead if I did. I couldn't let that happen.

DEWDROP: Cert.

CERT: Give me a kiss.

DEWDROP: What? No.

CERT: Come on, I'm dying. You can't give a dying brotha a kiss?

DEWDROP: You're not dying, Cert. I won't let you.

CERT: I don't think this is something you can control.

DEWDROP: Yes, it is.

Fuck! I knew I shouldn't have let you come with me.

CERT: It ain't your fault, Dewdrop. I wanted to come.

DEWDROP: You're not going to die.

CERT: I need you to do something for me.

DEWDROP: What is it?

CERT: I need you to keep your promise.

DEWDROP: What promise?

CERT: If I died here, you'd kill me yourself.

DEWDROP: I can't do that.

CERT: Ya gotta do it, Fly Girl. Please.

DEWDROP: Fucking motherfucker!

CERT: Yo, you don't kill me now, then blood-sucking undead me is gonna come back and, fo sho, kill the shit outta you.

DEWDROP: I drop Long Tooths all the time, Cert. I think I can handle keeping myself from getting bitten by yo' ugly ass.

CERT: I'm ugly now, huh? Damn. You like to kick a brotha when he's down.

Dewdrop. Seriously now. I don't wanna become whatever it is they become. Fuck that.

DEWDROP: Don't make me do this.

CERT: And seriously I'm gonna be mad dangerous too if you don't take me out. I'm already badass as it is, you just saw what I did to Boss 2K. Can you imagine me with some Longtooth powers? Shit, son, I'd make the devil piss his pants.

DEWDROP: Maybe you ain't gonna turn evil.

CERT: Dewdrop, come on. It ain't like I wanna die. Don't make this hard.

DEWDROP: Cert.

CERT: What is this? You're crying. For me.

DEWDROP: Of course I am.

CERT: And all this while I thought you didn't care.

DEWDROP: Of course I care.

CERT: Then prove it.

(DEWDROP *kisses* CERT.)

CERT: Damn, girl. Why you gotta be gay?

DEWDROP: I don't know. Why you gotta go get bitten by Boss 2K and now make me have to kill you?

CERT: Touche', my chigga. Touche'.

Just keep your promise, aight?

DEWDROP: Alright...

(DEWDROP *suddenly begins strangling* CERT. *It is not an easy death. He struggles, but dies. After he loses consciousness, she sees his wooden sword. She picks it up and slowly pushes the tip of it into his heart for good measure. As she pulls the weapon out, a song like* Amazing *by Kanye West begins playing.*)

Four

(*A weaponless* DEWDROP *wanders the streets of Brooklyn with the song still playing in the background. She's considerably weak, but still pushing forward.*)

(*As she crosses the stage, we see projections of Brooklyn buildings go by, it takes exactly one minute in real-time to cross.*)

(As she makes it to the other end, the stage has transformed into The Brooklyn Bridge.)

(Projection: CHAPTER FIVE: THE SHIT HITS THE FAN)

(Projection: Brooklyn Bridge, Brooklyn)

(Lights come up on a group of LONG TOOTHS *wielding swords and other martial arts weapons. They surround* DEWDROP. *We hear them growl.)*

LONG TOOTH: No one gets outta Brooknam alive!

DEWDROP: Come on, muthafuckahs. Bring it.

(They attack. A song like the original "Thought at Work" by The Roots begin playing.)

(This is an amazing and very physical battle. Though they outnumber her, her skills and determination prevail.)

(After disarming and stealing one of the LONG TOOTH'S *swords,* DEWDROP *vanquishes her attackers.)*

*(*LADY SNOWFLAKE *enters as the final* LONG TOOTH *is killed. She begins clapping.)*

LADY SNOWFLAKE: Moshi, moshi, motherfucker.

DEWDROP: Sally.

LADY SNOWFLAKE: Why so glum, chum? What's with the long face?

DEWDROP: What's with the long tooth?

LADY SNOWFLAKE: Good one.

DEWDROP: You're not her. You're not really her.

LADY SNOWFLAKE: Oh, I'm not, am I? I'm not the first girl you ever loved? The first girl whose name you scribbled in your notebook with hearts circled all around it?

DEWDROP: Shut up.

LADY SNOWFLAKE: I'm not the first girl you ever let

take you to heaven and back with just the use of a
tongue and a forefinger?

DEWDROP: Stop.

LADY SNOWFLAKE: What? Too graphic for you? Okay,
how's this for PG-13? Am I not the first girl you left
dying in the streets five years ago because your chicken
shit ass wasn't brave enough to open the goddamn car-
door to let me in? "Open the door. Open the fucking
door." That meant for you to let me in, not for you to
drive away, ya dumb cunt.

DEWDROP: Don't call me that.

LADY SNOWFLAKE: And secondly. Oh yes, bitch, there's
a secondly. Secondly, to follow up your utter failures at
being my greatest love, it took you over a half-decade
to finally come back to get me some revenge. Shit,
bitch, I got cans of Spam that rot faster than that. And
Spam, as you might know since you're fucking Filipino
and all, takes a goddamn long time to fucking rot.
   You abandoned me, Dew. And the truth is, I'm
glad I'm what I am now. And not because of the
superpowers or my amazing kinkilicous outfits.
I'm glad cause if I weren't, that shit you done to me
woulda hurt pretty fucking bad. So, see, there's a boon
to not having a soul, little Samurai. It makes living life
a lot easier. Ain't that a something?

DEWDROP: Stay back.

LADY SNOWFLAKE: But, worry not, I'm not mad at ya.
No way. You gave me a gift tonight afterall.

I'm the new Kingsborough King. And it's all because of
you.

DEWDROP: Goddamn it.

LADY SNOWFLAKE: Let me look at you, baby. I'm glad
to be able to see that gorgeous face of yours again. That
face I once loved. A face that once loved me.

DEWDROP: Don't—

LADY SNOWFLAKE: You and I were meant to be queens, baby girl. We were meant to rule the world, not stand here on this old bridge fighting like a pair of some sad samurai. Let me give you what you deserve.

DEWDROP: You're not you.

LADY SNOWFLAKE: Oh, it's me. Every fine fiber, every delectable inch. I'm that girl you loved and lost and now see again. And I'm asking you—girl who once broke my heart—are you really going to kill me?

DEWDROP: Sally, stay /away from me.

LADY SNOWFLAKE: Shhhhhhhhhh.

(LADY SNOWFLAKE *calmly approaches* DEWDROP. DEWDROP *lowers her weapon as* LADY SNOWFLAKE *leans in to kiss her.* DEWDROP *reciprocates. It's a very loving moment.*)

(*Abruptly,* DEWDROP *shoves her away.*)

DEWDROP: NO. I won't be one of you.

LADY SNOWFLAKE: I'm not here to give you that choice, baby girl.

(DEWDROP *raises her weapon again.*)

LADY SNOWFLAKE: Oh, baby, I like it when you play "hard to get". Cause, baby, I'm gonna getcha.

DEWDROP: I'm no longer afraid to die.

LADY SNOWFLAKE: Good. Cause I'm gonna kill ya hard, slow, and sexy-like.

DEWDROP: Correction, bitch, you mean you're gonna try...

(*And now, in the best girl-fight ever to be seen on a N Y stage [to a song like Kanye West's* Welcome to Heartbreak*],* DEWDROP *and* SNOWFLAKE *go at it Kung Fu style. Think the fight in* Crouching Tiger, Hidden

Dragon *except even better. And live. And more awesome.)*

(The fight begins with one slow methodical circle. As the fighters find their in, they suddenly rush at each other. The fight goes back and forth with breaks in between to address wounds, but LADY SNOWFLAKE *in the end gets the advantage when she disarms* DEWDROP.*)*

(As DEWDROP *lies on the ground,* LADY SNOWFLAKE *gives* DEWDROP *a kiss on her forehead. She then goes to bite her, but right before she can sink her teeth,* DEWDROP *reverses the hold and impales* LADY SNOWFLAKE. LADY SNOWFLAKE *looks at her wound and falls.)*

*(*DEWDROP *somberly stands above her fallen love.* LADY SNOWFLAKE, *though not dead, is very helpless at this point.)*

*(*DEWDROP *raises her blade, but still does not have the strength to finish* SALLY *off. So instead she holds her and looks up into the sky. She notices that the sun is about to rise.)*

DEWDROP: Look, baby, the sun's coming up.
It's almost over now.
It's almost over.
I love you.

(As the sun begins to rise...)

(Cut to...)

(Video sequencE: A video is played showing DEWDROP *and* SALLY *slowdancing to a song like* I Never Dreamed *by The Cookies in their kitchen.)*

DEWDROP: Are you still reading?

LADY SNOWFLAKE: What? I like to read.

DEWDROP: Come here.

LADY SNOWFLAKE: Why?

DEWDROP: Dance with me.

LADY SNOWFLAKE: You're a dork.

DEWDROP: Come on.

LADY SNOWFLAKE: You want me to dance with you, baby girl?

DEWDROP: Always.

(They try several bad attempts at turns and dips. They laugh. They are happy. They are in love. Lights fade on this image.)

(Title card: END OF PART ONE)

END OF PLAY!

(...Oh, but wait just a minute...)

(As the audience is exiting the house after an amazing curtain call sequence, a video begins playing on the back screen.)

(It's a film of DEWDROP finally arriving back home after her battle with LADY SNOWFLAKE.)

(As she enters her old and scarce apartment, we see a figure standing by the window staring outside. He begins speaking...)

MAYOR PENA: So you killed Boss 2K...

DEWDROP: The fuck you doing in my apartment, chigga?

MAYOR PENA: Ain't everyday you hear about a Shogun gettin' whacked. You must be some kinda supah Soul Samurai.

DEWDROP: Who are you?

(He turns and we see that it's Ralph Pena A K A MAYOR PENA.)

MAYOR PENA: Oh, me? I'm Mayor Pena, the new Shogun of Manhattan.

(We see he's holding a katana of his own.)

MAYOR PENA: And I'm here to lay the smackdown on your sweet ass.

(DEWDROP *smiles as she picks up her sword.*)

DEWDROP: Correction, bitch, you mean you're gonna try...

(*The two charge at one another.*)

(*Their weapons clash.*)

(*Black out.*)

(*Title Card: To be continued...*)

CPSIA information can be obtained
at www.ICGtesting.com
Printed in the USA
LVOW10s1723130917
548612LV00010B/871/P

9 780881 454512